The Man Who Never Was

The Man Who Never Was

Peter E. Murphy

Copyright©2018 Peter E. Murphy
All Rights Reserved

Published by Unsolicited Press
Portland, Oregon
www.unsolicitedpress.com

No part of this book may be reproduced or transmitted in any form or by any means without written permission from the publisher or author.

Printed in the United States of America.

Attention schools and businesses: for discounted copies on large orders, please contact the publisher directly.

ISBN: 978-1-947021-61-7

CONTENTS

Preface	7
One Plus One Equals One	11
The Last of Peter Murphy	13
Search For a Bent Twig	15
The Man Who Never Was	17
All That Lia Ever Wanted	19
The Escape	21
Death in Vienna	23
A Little Ignorance	25
Target: Eva	27
The Big Fish	29
Pay Now, Pray Later	31
Games of Death	33
If This Be Treason	35
To Kill an Albatross	37
Things Dead and Done	39
The Perfect Game	41
In Memory of Davos	43
Drop by Drop	45
I Take This Woman	47
Attributions	49
Acknowledgments	50
About the Author	51
About the Press	52

PREFACE

The Man Who Never Was was a failed TV show from the late Sixties whose protagonist was a spy named Peter Murphy. The poems in this collection borrow the titles of the show's 19 episodes to explore identities, politics, lies (Sorry, that's redundant) and personal mythology while shamelessly punning and quoting from Murphy's Law, The Peter Principle, The Dropkick Murphys and the English post-punk-godfather of Goth, Peter Murphy. If that weren't enough, the poems test the reader's patience by alluding to celebrities such as Lance Armstrong, Robert Blake, James Gandolfini, Greta Garbo, Samuel Johnson, Dee Dee Ramone, Jada Pinkett-Smith and others born on the author's birthday, September 18, as well as Daj Hammarskjöld and Jimi Hendrix who died on that same date. What a mess.

The Man Who Never Was

ONE PLUS ONE EQUALS ONE

> *The buddy system is essential to survival; it gives the enemy*
> *somebody else to shoot at.*

I was canned from sustainable employment
after years of labor. Someone
was working what shouldn't be worked,
blaming me, scratching my name in triplicate
on carbonless forms. I suspected
another Peter Murphy at work here,
one who intentionally botches things,
and me getting the blame and the claims
on my salary and the threatening messages
in my electronic mail.
I discovered the backslider buried deep
in the guts of the company
where he started in the mail room and stayed.
I looked around his slovenly cubicle,
decided to get tough.
My name is Peter Murphy, I said,
and you are wrecking my life.
When this other Peter Murphy shook his head,
I couldn't get over how much he looked
like me: same red eyes, blotched face, gray beard.
Same bad posture.
This man too, defeated—
Perhaps there's a third Peter Murphy,

he suggested, who's ruining both our lives.
We worked together, uncovered a whole department
where everyone is named Peter Murphy,
each one enjoying the benefits of full employment,
the company of his peers,
the tenure provided by this union.
Each one fucking up the works,
his job, guaranteed for life.

THE LAST OF PETER MURPHY

> *His lyrics, sometimes pretentious, bounce from profound*
> *philosophical statements to incomprehensible semantic fields.*

I am an alien ineligible to become President,
a mule horse grazing on the grounds of public policy.

I majored in demoralization studies, couldn't distinguish
God's sup from gossip, passing from passive. I avoided

assisted living, managed care, pre-existing conditions.
I survived as an economic refugee from a non-symbiotic
    culture.

I wanted to become a manifesto, to be read between
the lines. More than a stick figure. More than a fiddler.

I endured a tepid war between history and silence,
the social constructions of the first world.

I didn't mind changing moveable type.
I titled my first book, *Autobiography of the Anonymous*.

I loved to pronounce *cache, ochre, pomegranate*, *Namibia*.
I learned to speak backwards, to pay the exorcist twice.

Forgive me. I don't want to live as an ancestor until I die. I unpeeled the apple and returned it to the snake.

SEARCH FOR A BENT TWIG

If I could drop dead right now, I'd be the happiest man alive.

I left my heart in Hartford 35 years ago.
She jumped out of the heated car in an argument
that burst into flame, and I drove
for decades before heading back.

I whirl into the Lifespan Hospital and gladhand
throngs of cutting-edge surgeons.
I see you, says admissions, bored, dead
slow to the traffic of metaphor which has carried me

to this room for emergencies. Are you smarter than
Miss America? I ask the cardio cutting open my chest.
Did you cheat on your boards? Your wife?
Will you unplug my heart if it's full,

empty it out the window like a tray of ashes?
Keep your legs crossed, you stupid sheet
he replies, and grunts to the hallway
where he slaps his cell to his ear

and says he's ahead of schedule,
should be somewhere soon. *Hospital sued
by 7 foot doctors. Iraqi head seeks arms.
Crack found on governor's daughter.*

Trouble is metaphor that won't stop when I turn it off,
that drips like blood on the upholstery of the Impala.
The Hartford Courant fades in the gurney next to me.
Trouble is, I'm fully compatible with dying.

THE MAN WHO NEVER WAS

I have mapped out a continent
and sent it back to confuse those who might follow.

Courtesy killed the cat
used to being kicked in the ribs,
thrown against a wall, mewing
I am so hungry I could eat the dates
off a calendar.

You want to cry?
Alcohol is the cause and solution
to all life's problems, burps
the cartoon father.
Beauty is in the eye of the beer holder.

I can't sleep, clowns will eat me.
Leave no turn unstoned, they chant
before courtesy smothers me again.
I drink, therefore I am, and I am
so hungry.

Kids eat free, a hotel advertises.
What I don't know is everything.
He say I mad, a girl complains
to the school, *'cause he get more pussy*
than I get dick.

Children make healthy snacks,
replies the board of education.
You want to cry?
No Eisensteins here,
the board president proclaims.

I am afraid of changing rooms.
I do not support the missionary position.
I cannot sleep and am always hungry.
Evolution is a lie.
I am afraid of trees, the horizon, the wilderness.

ALL THAT LIA EVER WANTED

If you get them by the balls, their hearts and minds will follow.

The man who never was is born
behind enemy lines on a farm where women
spray their lawn with grape seed extract
to keep gallows birds from alighting.

He has avoided prosecution, authorized use,
the missionary position.
He would love to recover his manliness
which dribbled out of him when his kid skin

popped in the back seat of a ride he hitched
to Rock…Rock…Rockaway Beach.
It is supposed to be new millennium,
but it is the same old new shit, shit, shit

he wakes to throwing up his life.
I would like to thank myself, he mocks,
and congratulate myself, and if I could,
I would pat myself on the back.

Put up your dukes, she startles him.
Are you a man or a louse, or is that redundant?
He would like to offer her his body.
Instead he backs away, apologizing.

My shelf life has expired, and I am
not committed to my original sins.
I am not ambitious. I don't want pieces
of the world. I... I... I...

What if there's an eclipse? she interrupts.
You little ice age-lost in action in a live impact area!
Is that all you can do? Repeat yourself?
Yourself?

THE ESCAPE

Mickey Mouse is a rat.

The man who never was
braces a jackhammer in his arms,
purses his pneumatic lips as it rumbles
between his legs crying *Harder! Harder!*

straining his muscles so when he lies
sleepless in his rented bed
his soft limbs quiver
through the barking night.

The construction site is struck
by a shakedown of made men
pointing nightmares at his chest,
each cocked, ready to go off.

*No more funny business for you,
Mr. Holy Smoke,* they threaten.
Should the world fail to fall apart,
fears the man who never was,

he will continue doing time
making rich men richer,
fabricating a history of good
others will extort.

The light pours from him
dim and out of breath,
like flowers and razors bleeding
from his lungs with no air apparent.

In comes the Don, *My people are nuts,*
he apologizes, releasing him to twirl in the wind.
Get back to work, and spare no expense,
the boss man bosses, *to save money on this one.*

DEATH IN VIENNA

He who does not mind his belly, will hardly mind anything else.

Opportunity killed the cats, time released
from the basement of block scheduling.
Lucky and Hungry starved grazing the air time
for attic access and mice accidents.

You want to cry?
I am what I haven't eaten, believes
the man who never was walking dead slow
against vanity releases and rip currents.

I don't need *need* he thinks as he stumbles
upon well fed comedians who cook
their lines from medium rare to well done.
Don't feed the models, Rochester warns

his stingy boss who plucks strings for a laugh.
My favorite animal is steak, the boss sauces a pink actress.
What's yours? Be careful, Rochester protests.
She will eat us out of porterhouse and home.

If you don't sleep on your stomach, can I?
The boss tries again.
If I said you had a beautiful body,
would you hold it against me?

Never eat more than you can lift, Rochester chastens.
The man who never was swipes a sweet
from a tray of pastries, his eye on a table of *crude-itties*
and *whores-do-orves*. And look out for Garbo!

the porter portends. She's gunning for thirteen years
of my life. Ask not what you can do for your country,
considers the man who never was, walking away
chewing his loot. Instead, ask what's for lunch

A LITTLE IGNORANCE

Nothing is as easy as it looks.

Higher education makes me hungry, moans
the man who never was. He hasn't finished
the first of his courses and he wants more,
and more of more.

I am fed up with institutional patriotism
which cannot put a table under my food.
I am tired of working, then not working.
I want to be the full of full employment.

The deans turn into offices. Their eyes
crispy microfiche in the cleavage
of unstacked reference librarians who love
their books so much they hold them to their chests.

I want to be alone.
I want electroshock and coffee.
I am so hungry I had my mouth sewn shut.
I want to be King Food, marauder of the buffet.

Financial circumstance displaces him into a shelter
in New Jersey where he downloads pictures
of a cheesesteak sandwich and emails them to his son
and bride freezing in St. Petersburg.

Son writes back as if he were a doctor,
Do not resuscitate.
I know better, thinks the man who never was,
but I want more of the past, and I want it now.

TARGET: EVA

Police begin campaign to run down jaywalkers.

Who rode the white horse?
ponders the dark girl with hiccups
who walks away from the man who never was,
wondering why he asked her that.

He stops another who carries canned fruit
ripe from the food line. History is a prison,
he proclaims. Man, she yells, get outta
my face or I'll fuck you up!

This must be my mother, he thinks,
surrounded by the children of instant esteem.
She sounds just like my mother.
He finds himself face down on the linoleum

surrounded by security which challenges
his adult admissions. Who are you?
they demand, tying his arms around his back.
He has no pass, no ID.

If he had a name it might be Special Ed.
It might be Fuck You.
Who's cutting high school drop outs in half?
he shouts. Why did the teacher strike idle kids?

Around them, an infestation
of blood-born *passengers* begins to light
on their interrogation, their soft skins,
their small boards of education.

Throw him out! insecurity decides, yelling,
Stay the hell away from here!
Why is trying the first step towards failure?
he screams back. Why was I never teacher's pet?

The man who never was maunders
from the busy pavement into the monopoly
of traffic where he becomes a fish swimming on fire
from one school to another.

THE BIG FISH

In Hollywood a marriage is a success if it outlasts milk.

The man who never was is afraid he will burn
in the dog light delivering take out. He is afraid
of witness protection, of bad stars and bastards
and Mr. Violence who answers the door with a knife

for his lecherous wife. I told her not to wander
'round in the dark, he jokes, as his wife gets
thrust with pokes. Maybe you'd like to poke
her too, he offers the clueless detectives

who show up to drool over her nude photos.
The man who never was carries a small chunk
of the Berlin Wall chipped from Checkpoint Charlie
before it went AWOL.

His heart, like the iron curtain, is a museum
of bright blood. He hopes the Chinese are happy
they still have their wall, despite détente
and disposable income and expiration dates.

I can't live on what I make the dead wife complains.
She likes to sleep with bank accounts—
Elvis, Chubby Checker. She slept Jerry
Lee Lewis who denied her child.

The man who never was would like a steady job,
insurance against disability, a house in the country.
Don't you find me attractive? the slain wife teases.
Maybe you and I could make a living.

Her life was intended for single use only,
protest her nine former husbands.
I lost 40 pounds in 2 months, she screams back
as he returns to his take away orders.

He fixes his bloodshot eyes on the wilderness.
He must deliver a birthday cake to Jonny Quest,
one funeral arrangement to Dag Hammarskjöld,
another to Jimi Hendrix.

PAY NOW, PRAY LATER

We've had your money now goodbye
We fleeced you good we bled you dry

The man who never was
buys his clothes and his casket
at a shop called Mommasville
where young women stow
their children in changing rooms
and slink out for a dusty at the bar.

All clowns have agendas,
warns the anti-clown community.
Just because they make people laugh
doesn't mean they're not out to get you.
You want to cry?
Every mother breeds new problems.

The man who never was
listens to the damned on compact disc,
insulated by a sleeve covering scars
gnawed into him as a gap child.
Nice cuppa tea, toasts his dead mum
browsing forever among the diddle-daddle.

Nature always sides with the hidden flaw.
Be careful what you wish for.

Whaddya want, Ma? he calls out,
a basic chucklehead with a handful of coins.
Everything is on sale here, she says.
Here, they hold nothing back.

GAMES OF DEATH

Home wasn't built in a day.

Opportunity is a prologue to sorrow,
realizes the man who never was,
caught in a fuss with the meat-fisted waitress
who refuses to bring him hash.

He wants to change his life, mine the gap
between poverty and hunger. He wants to peddle
his childhood, a grueling 2,274 miles through the Alps
of Brooklyn and Bordeaux. He wants to jump in a lake

and come out dry. So he sits at the counter
where nothing adds up, where the waitress says, sorry,
I didn't know you were here, and he thinks me too,
paging the want ads searching for need—

Dog for sale: eats anything, fond of children.
For Rent: 6 room hated apartment.
3-year old teacher for preschool, smacks included.
Free puppies, part shepherd, part dog, speaks German.

Mr. and Mrs. Beautiful sit with their brood
in a window booth, lifting food carefully
to their mouths with the finely sharpened
tines of their forks.

Why go elsewhere to be cheated. Come here first.
Stock up and save. Limit: one.
Man, honest. Will take anything.
Experienced Mom will care for you.

He feels like a slow-working insect digging
out of the soil, crawling to their booth on his knees.
Will you be my mother? he begs.
The art of parenting is the art of lying to children.

IF THIS BE TREASON

*The only thing more accurate than incoming enemy fire is
incoming friendly fire.*

Property is theft, laments the man who never was
because he owns none, wondering how
the huge oceanfront homes occupy themselves
when they are not sheltering their families from taxes.

Capitalism is not love, his mother taught him
before breaking up. An ounce of image is worth
a pound of incompetence in any economy,
her own life sprouted from a bottle of gin.

I've been bamboozled, complains the iron curtain.
Give me back my wall and my economy
and my resources and my gray, gray shelf lives
and my health care and my parades and my Leningrad.

I want my Leningrad!
Give me my masses whose hope turned their hoes
to soil up an empire which could feed itself and march
and keep on marching and feeding and making.

> *Man exploits man, each according to his ability.*
> *Company announces chair leaving.*
> *Miners refuse to work after death.*

Make me a tomb, Goodyear orders
the man who never was, who hoists a brown bag
over his shoulder, the storefront advertising
We Delivery! on its paned glass.

TO KILL AN ALBATROSS

When a man tells you that he got rich through hard work,
ask him whose?

The man who never was
lumbers up the stairs to the condominiums
where he will do maximum work
for minimum wage.

If he had a name it might be Peter Murphy
converting punk to dust.
It might be Garry Morgan tramping
through Wales looking for his head.

He mops himself
into an electrical room where the doors are alarmed
and the buttons depressed.
He is afraid of embellished charges, of adult emissions.

He is afraid of occupational language,
of press releases and masking tape.
He is afraid he will deplete his dialogue bank—
When all his words are exhausted he will die.

Around his neck hangs the figure
of a smaller man chained to a piece of wood.
If this man had a name it might be Jesus Christ.

It might be Albert Ross.

The man who never was dreams his body
commutes from home to office bearing a tie, a jacket,
a brief case of important papers. And in the suburbs,
a wife, a child or two, a dog that does not bite.

THINGS DEAD AND DONE

We didn't lose the game; we just ran out of time.

The man who never was lies awake
dreaming in the third person.

Sleeping is no laughing matter, he thinks
and rises sleepless from his aching bed.

He has become a waking hallucination
larger and sloppier than slang.

At first his brain aches, then freezes,
and sometimes a single section will implode

into disorder and oddness.
There is little sequence—

> *Nothing improves with love*
> *Death has no calories*

> *Sex cuts efficiency*
> *Families cause loneliness, feelings of isolation*

—that would have been impossible
if he had been able to sleep.

Can everything be used at random,
he wonders, and wrenched into song?

THE PERFECT GAME

*Lying increases the creative faculties, expands the ego,
and lessens the frictions of social contacts.*

It's a beautiful thing to have money,
prescribes Mr. Nobody to his son.
I guess you ain't got too much beauty,
you should buy yourself some.

So the man who never was drags himself
up from the curb where he spent
another bloody night peeing in place of a bed
and maunders to the museum of bad ideas

where the Celtic crosses are molded styrofoam
which the guards guard and will not let him touch.
You live a life of unrelieved insignificance,
he tells himself. If there's such a thing as an afterlife,

it better be better than Cardiff. This from the drunk
who thirty years before flung himself from the top
of a construction site into a university where even
the nude encounter group enforced a dress code.

Nothing for nothing you stupid sheet, the university
scolded. You wanna come in you gotta pay.
See this hand? the Dean of *Studnets* challenged.

This is the hand that's gonna slap you

as he palm-dashed his cheek with the other. Lying's fine,
but that hurts, complained the man who never was,
turning his cheek from one punch line to the next: Did
you hear about the cannibal eaten by clowns?

Never trust an exile, warns the Marks and Sparks oracle.
    Who are you? What do you mean by love?
Never do card tricks in front of your poker buddies.
    What do you believe and why do you believe it?

The last round of drinks is on the house as he crawls
off his wagon to climb after them. A penny saved is a
    penny,
he says, which is why his income is disposable.
The more money people make, the less they sing.

IN MEMORY OF DAVOS

*Nothing fixes a thing so intensely in the memory
as the wish to forget it.*

The man who never was was a child
of Munchausen syndrome, swathed
in velcro-like gauze until his blistered skin
peeled away from his broken mother.

He was never a Jonny in search of a quest
till he rummaged through all the houses
of his development, finding only a gossip
of neighbors, trying to comprehend why the dates

on his calendar go from prime numbers to primeval.
If he had a name, he thinks,
it might be Open Mike, though none of his thoughts
have been spoken, none of his words audible.

His crude futures complain, Why can't we
just not do nothing? The man who never was
gets off in the dog dark and tries to walk home
without stopping at a place where men stop to perish.

He wants to be alone in a grand hotel
and sleep without dreaming of the condition
of his conditions. Mothers are engines,

he realizes, rumbling on fool power.

He turns into a gentleman's club in a strip mall,
a club where nostalgia serves drinks
on the house, a club where not even the dead
can disturb him.

DROP BY DROP

*So kiss me, I'm shitfaced and i'm soaked and i'm soiled
and brown in the trousers.*

The man who never was always kept a supply
of stimulant handy in case he saw a snake,
which he also kept handy. When he read

about the evils of drinking, he gave up reading.
If you're coasting, she scolded, *you're going down hill.*
she'd leave him, she threatened, if he didn't try
        something else.

So he switched from 100 proof vodka to eighty.
You never do sober what you say you'd do drunk, she carped.
No drinking plan ever survives contact with the enemy.

You can't break even. You can't win. You can't even lose.
Nothing is impossible for the person
who doesn't have to do it herself.

Drunkenness knows no barriers. Bacchus hath drowned
more men than Neptune.
Work is the curse of the drinking classes.

He dove when he drank, but he couldn't swim.
Now all these years he's had nothing to live on

but food and water. He wants to believe

he is having a good time. At least I had something
to blame myself on, he muses. These days
he tumbles from bed to verse.

I TAKE THIS WOMAN

*Forget everything you think you know about Peter Murphy.
Tear it up and then tape it all back together with your eyes
closed.*

Hitler toes the rubber, throws
a curveball at his original ax causing
a barmaid in South Wales to hold out

free drinks to Mr. Nobody who fails
to stop despite red lights and stolen jeeps.
Bistro? offers Paris on his return trip

on a hospital ship tipped up with injuries
to make him well enough to change
his life, take the Welsh maid as wife

and detour through delayed openings
into citizen banks, babyland and free air.
No wonder nothing works, curses his son,

the man who never was, pursing his portfolio
riddled by Samuel B. Dictionary who advised
him to write only for money.

*Your manuscript is both good and original,
but the part that is good is not original*

> *and the part that is original is not good.*

This should be the beginning, laments
the man who never was. Instead it's the end: Lightning!
Fireworks! Closing music. Caterers on the credits.

> *Deaf mute gets new hearing in killing.*
> *War dims hope for peace.*
> *Milk drinkers turning to powder.*

You want to cry?

> *Repent: The Lord kills.*

ATTRIBUTIONS

The epigraphs on the these pages are attributed to the following:

11 – Murphy's War Laws
13 – Said Sukkarieh
15 – Samuel Goldwyn
17 – Mr. Nobody
19 – Theodore Roosevelt
21 – Anonymous
23 – Samuel Johnson
25 – Murphy's Laws
27 – Newspaper headline (Apocryphal)
29 – Rita Rudner
31 – The Damned
33 – Jane Sherwood Ace
35 – Murphy's War Laws
37 – Don Marquis
39 – Vince Lombardi
41 – Clare Boothe Luce
43 – Michel de Montaigne
45 – The Dropkick Murphys
47 – Metropolis Records

ACKNOWLEDGMENTS

Cake Magazine (Lancaster University): "Drop by Drop"

Chest, The Journal of American Chest Physicians: "Search For a Bent Twig"

The Edison Review: "One Plus One Equals One," "The Last of Peter Murphy"

Hayden's Ferry Review: "The Escape," "Target: Eva"

The Journal: "Games of Death"

The Literary Review: "To Kill an Albatross"

Nightsun: "The Man Who Never Was"

Protest Poems: "If This Be Treason"

The Seventh Quarry (Swansea, Wales): "Pay Now, Pray Later"

Tiferet: "Things Dead and Done"

U.S. 1 Worksheets: "A Little Ignorance"

ABOUT THE AUTHOR

Peter E. Murphy was born in Wales and grew up in New York City where he operated heavy equipment, managed a nightclub and drove a taxi. He is the author of ten books and chapbooks including *Stubborn Child*, a finalist for the Paterson Poetry Prize, and *Looking for Thelma*, winner of the inaugural Wilt Nonfiction Chapbook Prize. He is the founder of Murphy Writing of Stockton University.

ABOUT THE PRESS

Unsolicited Press is a small press founded in 2012 and is based in Portland, Oregon. The team seeks to publish exemplerary fiction, poetry, and creative nonfiction. Learn more at www.unsolicitedpress.com.

www.ingramcontent.com/pod-product-compliance
Lightning Source LLC
Chambersburg PA
CBHW052106110526
44591CB00013B/2373